Codependency:

The 30-Day Break Free Guide

Learn How to Recognize and Eliminate Your Codependent Programming

by Stanley Murdock

Table of Contents

Selected Amazon Reviews

„What I like about the book is that it comes from the personal experience. It's not just a list of general guidelines, but one can sense that the author himself had to go through the whole process of letting loose. Thus, there's the actual plan taking your from recognizing the problem to resolving it, showing you the usual patterns of codependent behavior. You will be advised on what steps to take in order to break free, to set goals to yourself, set boundaries and "stop the drama". Eventually it will all lead up to "a healthy balance in different aspects of life". The author says: "Finally, you should learn to love and live again." Such inspirational words!"

„This is a good book for any beginners to the subject who feel they have been living a codependent lifestyle. The author has set up a 30-day plan to help you get over your codependency issues one by one. There is an issue to address for every day. The areas covered include setting boundaries, building self-esteem, taking good care of yourself and becoming a better communicator. There are also sections on enabling, self-care, financial responsibility, and goal setting. This guide will help you to take better control of your life, and to assure that you are in much healthier relationships. This book is quick, to the point and helpful."

„This book directs in bringing an optimistic transformation in our living and our relationship. This one-month guide helps in changing our approach to life and guides towards betterment in a gradual mode. The author has kept it straightforward and concise."

Introduction

Are you wondering if you are in a codependent relationship? Do you want to get out of it? Do you want to know how codependency affects you? Is there a way to prevent codependency? Is there a way to cure it? If you think you are in a codependent relationship and is curious on how you could turn it around, then this book is for you.

In this book, you will learn about what codependency really is and how it can affect your life and behaviour. This book will guide you in performing an awareness exercise and codependency exercises. These exercises will help you in regaining control over your life and will save you from being judgmental. You have to be honest with yourself all the time and have self-awareness. This book also contains mantras that you can recite over and over again to remind yourself that you are not a worthless person. Ask yourself why you do what you do, and start changing your behaviour. Set yourself free and stop being a victim of a codependent relationship.

Live your life to the fullest and transform yourself into a new you.

I wrote this book because I have experienced codependency. Working really hard to get out of that codependent relationship has been a challenge for me. It was a very depressing relationship wherein I lost my self and treated my partner like a god and my world. It is a relationship which I do not want to experience again. The guidelines I included in this book taught me how to stand on my own and become independent. I have realized that I have to love myself first before others. I decided to make this book to help people out there who are in a codependent relationship but cannot do anything about it. Start encouraging yourself that you can do it and realize that your opinion about yourself is more important than what other people say or think about you. This book is for people who want to set themselves free and be the person they want to be. Take the risk and learn to accept reality and be free.

Each chapter will expand your knowledge about a codependent relationship and a step by step process you can do every day to help you cope up with codependency. Each chapter will help you let go of the fears in the past and the future so you can live your present life to the fullest. Every chapter will open your heart and mind to forgive and forget.

With your passion and intention to get out of a codependent relationship you will find yourself free in just a wave of your hand and blink of your eyes. You will regain control over your life and people will start to see the new you. Start living and have a great life. So turn the page and begin your transformation now!

Day 1: Understand What Codependency Really Is

If you often find yourself making sacrifices for the sake of your partner while you do not get anything in return, then perhaps you are in a codependent relationship. It is a behavioral pattern wherein you become dependent on the approval of your partner for your identity and self-worth. It makes you feel trapped and vulnerable. It also makes you anxious.

The first step you have to take in order to regain control over your life is to understand what codependency really is. According to experts, one of the major signs of codependency is a loss of sense of purpose. When you find your whole world revolving around your partner, you may be codependent. Another sign is when you find yourself spending a lot of energy and time trying to conform to the wishes of your partner or trying to change them.

Dr. Scott Wetzler, chief of the psychology division at the Albert Einstein College of Medicine, said that codependent relationships involve unhealthy degrees of clinginess. It also involves individuals who rely on their partner for fulfillment. Researchers also suggest that those who grew up with neglectful or emotionally abusive parents are more likely to be in codependent relationships. They often replay their childhood pattern that is full of development gaps.

Day 2: Perform Awareness Exercises

Co-dependents are not flimsy people. In fact, a lot of co-dependents are capable and intelligent. This is why you have to keep an open mind. Just because you are able to do your job or study does not mean that you do not have codependency. Once you confirm that you are a codependent, you have to practice this exercise with honesty, self-openness, and humility.

To perform an awareness exercise, answer the following questions honestly:

Do you waste time getting anxious about what others think of you?

Do you always try to please people, so you can feel happy?

Do you tend to analyze the lives of other people?

Do you get anxious when you are not able to control situations?

Do you do and say what you believe others want you to do and say?

Do you attempt to control the behavior of others so that you can gain a peace of mind?

Do you have a hard time confronting issues and speaking up?

Do you blame others for the way you feel?

Do your mood levels follow the mood levels of other people?

Do you prefer to listen to other people than to listen to your own self?

Do you always find yourself saying 'yes' when you actually want to say 'no'?

Do you do everything for others and then become upset when they do not do anything for you?

Do you put the needs of other people before yours?

Do you expect other people to provide you with happiness rather than create it for yourself?

Be honest with yourself. Refrain from being judgmental. You need to practice self-awareness so you can finally overcome codependency.

Day 3: Release Codependency Exercises

Codependency exercises are important if you want to regain control over your life. Once you find out your problem areas, you have to understand why you do what you do, so you can finally change your behavior. To change your behavior, start by changing your beliefs. To change your beliefs, you need to find the source of your issues and turn the unconscious into conscious.

Return to the previous exercise. Read the statements where you answered 'yes' and figure out which ones brought you the most pain. Rate their level of pain from 1 to 10, 10 being the most painful. Then, rewrite the list, starting from the statements with the highest level of pain to the statements with the lowest level of pain.

When you are done, reflect on your list and ask yourself why you do the things that you do. Allow yourself to feel the pain without judging yourself or being fearful. You will eventually get the answers that you need from your infinite inner wisdom.

Day 4: Recite Independency Mantras

Now that you have found and dealt with the root causes of your issues, you can recite independency mantras that can help you remind yourself of your worth. These sample mantras can be recited in the morning before you start your day or in the evening before you go to sleep. Write down your mantras so that you will remember them.

"I am my own source of validation"

Oftentimes, people rely on others for validation. They even turn to social media to gain the attention and approval of their peers. However, you should realize that what you think of yourself is much more important than what others think of you. After all, it is your life and experiences. So, it is up to you to approve and encourage yourself.

"I am responsible for my self-fulfillment."

A lot of people find happiness in other people, their jobs, the money in their bank account, or the size and price of their properties. They only feel fulfilled when others admire them for the car they drive, how much money they make, and how big their houses are. However, you should realize that you are the sole source of your self-fulfillment. You cannot be genuinely happy if you have material goods or titles and yet still feel empty. You need to find the purpose of your life and follow your passions.

Day 5: Rewrite Your Script Exercise

Next, rewrite your script exercises so you can have a more empowered way of life. It is not easy to form new habits. However, if you have a clear plan, it would be easier for you to start and follow through. Force yourself to get out of your comfort zone so you can achieve growth.

Again, you should go back to your first list of statements. Then, you should go to your list of independency mantras. Choose statements and mantras that you feel go together. For example, if you agree with the statement that pertains to you saying 'yes' when you want to say 'no', pair it with the mantra reminding you that you are in control of your life.

Rewrite your script and make it more positive. So, instead of merely saying 'yes' when you want to say 'no', you can evaluate yourself first and listen to your emotions. If your inner self is telling you to say 'no', then you should say 'no'.

Day 6: Practice Detachment

Codependents have an unhealthy attachment to their partners. They do not have normal feelings, such as liking people, feeling connected with others, or being concerned about issues. They are overly involved. At times, they may even become hopelessly entangled.

Codependents are often excessively preoccupied or worried about their partners. They may also become reactionaries as well as caretakers to the individuals around them. They may become too dependent emotionally, as well as become obsessed with the idea of controlling everything around them.

Codependents need to get detached, which involves releasing themselves from the people they love. They have to physically, mentally, and emotionally get away from the unhealthy entanglements they have with the lives of other people. They have to start being responsible for their own selves and stop worrying about the problems that are not theirs or the situations that they cannot control.

They have to live in the present and allow things to naturally unfold. They have to let go of the regrets or fears they have about the past and the future so that they can make the most of their present.

Day 7: Do Not Get Blown About by Every Wind

Codependents are usually reactionaries. They react with guilt, anger, shame, hurt, worry, fury, desperation, depression, and self-hate. They also react with anxiety and fear, which often causes them so much pain.

To overcome codependency, you need to stop reacting to everything. This includes the feelings, problems, thoughts, and behaviors of other people. You should stop reacting to whatever they may be thinking, doing, or feeling.

Instead, you should focus on your own self. You should react to your own thoughts, feelings, actions, and problems. In addition, you should refrain from treating everything like a crisis. Otherwise, you will be in perpetual panic mode.

Stop reacting to everything that comes to your awareness. If you live your life reacting to the lives, problems, successes, desires, and faults of other people, you will diminish your self-esteem. This would cause you to sink even lower and spiral out of control.

Hence, you should learn to control yourself. Learn to figure out when you need to have a reaction and when you need to just let things go. Keep in mind that not everything that happens need to have an equivalent reaction.

Day 8: Set Yourself Free

Codependents are often controllers. They nag, scream, lecture, beg, cry, coerce, bribe, accuse, overprotect, provoke, entrap, seduce, and do other things that can be too extreme for their partners. They may go over the top and show huge gestures and then get upset when their partners do not give them the same level of validation and attention.

They may also create drama and treat every little issue as a big deal. In addition, they may try to do everything they can just to get the results they want, even if that means manipulating or completely changing their partners. In other words, they may no longer act normal and healthy.

If you find yourself having irrational thoughts and doing things that you normally do not do, you should stop in your tracks. Take a deep breath and really evaluate your behavior. Your obsession with your partner and your relationship may cause you to lose sight of what is real and important. Thus, you need to set yourself free by taking a break. You do not have to end the relationship or go away.

You just have to stop your unhealthy pattern or routine.

Day 9: Eliminate the Victim

Consider the following scenario: A woman was married an alcoholic man. Every night he goes to the local bars to get drunk. Then, his wife drives across town to look for him and bring him home. She feels sorry and concerned about him. She becomes the rescuer.

Once they get home, her feelings of concern turn into feelings of anger. She starts to scold him for being an alcoholic. She expects him to change his ways and be more responsible for his actions. She becomes the persecutor.

Afterwards, she feels sorry for herself. She feels helpless, ashamed, and desperate. After everything she has done for her husband, why does he treat her this way? She feels like a victim of life and of circumstance. She becomes the victim.

This is the usual pattern of a codependent. They feel the need to take care of their partners or to rescue them from themselves. Then, they feel upset at the behaviors of their partners and their repeated failure at making changes. They soon become frustrated because they do not get their desired outcome. Eventually, they start to break down and feel that they do not deserve what is happening to them.

If the scenario seems familiar to you and you see yourself in the woman in the story, then it is time to make a change. Instead of taking care of other people, you have to take care of yourself and your needs. You can only eliminate the victim if you do not create it in the first place.

Day 10: Undependence

A lot of people, especially women, tend to feel incomplete without a relationship. This is why they put up with their partners even though they become abusive and unstable. They stay in the relationship even though it means they have to do all the work and provide for their family. They want to leave because they are not happy, but at the same time, they also feel that they cannot live without their partners.

In essence, they cannot stand on their own and face the aloneness. They do not think that they can take care of themselves, and they may not even think that they want to. They want to have somebody, no matter what the risk or cost is.

According to Colette Dowling, this is what is referred to as The Cinderella Complex. Codependents seem to be helpless, fragile, powerful, or sturdy. However, all of them are needy, frightened, and vulnerable. They are just like children who wanted to be cared for and loved.

If you want to overcome your codependency, you have to aim for undependence and start to examine the ways you are financially and emotionally dependent on others. You have to take care of yourself whether you are in a relationship that you wish to continue or in a relationship that you wish to get out of. Dowling suggests that you do it with courageous vulnerability or feeling scared but still doing it anyway.

Day 11: Live Your Life

Codependents often get involved in the business of other people. So, if you want to get over your codependency, you should tend to your own affairs. This is the fastest way to be happy and sane.

Once you have detached from your partner or the people around you, you are left on your own. This is the time when you need to take responsibility for yourself. Do not blame anyone for any unfortunate circumstance that you experienced.

Take time to reflect on your behavior. You may realize that you have become so wrapped up in your partner that you forgot how to live and enjoy your own life. You may have experienced so much emotional distress that you have come to believe that you do not have a life.

You must realize that this is not true and that you are more than your problems. You have a great life that you should start living. Now that you are no longer solely focused on your partner and your relationship, you can start to focus on your interests, hobbies, and goals.

Day 12: Have a Love Affair with Your Own Self

A lot of codependents have low self-worth. They do not feel good about themselves. They do not like themselves and they do not even consider loving themselves.

Even worse, they tend to hate everything about themselves, including their appearance and body. They think that they are stupid, untalented, and incompetent. They also believe that they are unlovable as well as their thoughts are inappropriate and wrong.

Codependents think that they are not important. So, even though their feelings are not wrong, they still think that they do not matter. They are convinced that their needs are not important.

In codependency, everything is linked to everything else. Hence, self-worth is linked to actions. This is what makes codependents problematic. Because they hate themselves, they think that it is wrong to actually take care of themselves. They do not say 'no' to others. They go extra miles to get the approval of other people.

To overcome your codependency, read the book Honoring the Self by Nathaniel Branden. It tells you how you can honor yourself by thinking independently, knowing what you need and want, and having an attitude of self-acceptance. It also tells you to stay committed to your right to exist as well as to live authentically among others.

Day 13: Learn about Acceptance

Sane and normal people accept reality. However, codependents have a hard time dealing with it. They do not know what to expect, especially when they are in a relationship with people who are alcoholics, drug addicts, gamblers, or criminals.

When bombarded by losses, problems, and change, they lose themselves. They lose emotional and financial security, and they put their health at risk. They even lose faith in their deity. They also lose love and respect in the people they love.

Oftentimes, the most painful loss that codependents experience is the loss of their dreams. When they lose their idealistic and hopeful expectations for their future, they have a hard time accepting it.

As a codependent, you cannot change until you accept your codependent characteristics. You have to accept that you do not have any power over people and circumstances. You have to accept who you are. You have to allow yourself to be fully aware of your actions and choices.

Day 14: Feel Your Feelings

Codependents often lose touch with their emotional selves. They may withdraw emotionally to avoid getting hurt. They believe that emotional vulnerability is dangerous. They also believe that hurt begets hurt and that nobody will care about them. So, they choose to play it safe and go away.

Codependents are also depressed, repressed, and oppressed. Most of them are able to tell quickly what other people are feeling, why they feel that way, and how long they have felt that way. They are also able to tell what these people are most likely going to do about their feelings.

Codependents spend a lot of time pondering how other people feel so that they can fix issues. They attempt to control the feelings of others. They do not want to hurt, upset, or offend anyone. They feel responsible for the feelings of other people yet they do not know how they feel themselves. If they ever find out how they feel, they are not able to fix their own issues. They do not take responsibility for their emotional selves.

To overcome your codependency, you have to deal with your own emotions and respond accordingly. You have to learn that having feelings is normal and that you should not feel bad about having them. You have to choose a healthy way to release your emotions. You can cry or keep a journal, for example.

Day 15: Express Anger

Anger is a natural reaction. Healthy people know that getting angry is a natural part of life. They express it and then they move on. Codependents, however, have a hard time dealing with anger. This is especially true when they live with people who are drug addicts or alcoholics. Anger becomes a huge part of their lives. In fact, it becomes their lives.

When their partner gets mad, they also get mad. Even when they do not yell and they pretend that they are not angry, they are still angry. They may make gestures or give looks that give them away. Their anger may suddenly explode like a bomb. For example, when an alcoholic man yells at his wife, his wife may respond in anger. However, after responding in anger, the wife may experience self-loathing. This is a usual pattern for codependents. They do not release their anger in a healthy way.

To overcome codependency, you can deal with anger by addressing the myths you have about it.

37

You have to feel the emotion and acknowledge the thoughts that come with it. You also have to evaluate the thinking that goes with your anger. Then, you should make a responsible decision about the actions that you have to take. Do not let anger control you. Express it and take responsibility for it.

Day 16: Know that You Can Actually Think

Most codependents rely on their partners for their decisions. "What do you think I should do?" is a common question asked by codependents. They do not trust their minds. They are indecisive all the time. Even simple decisions like where to eat for dinner makes them anxious. They become overwhelmed with major decisions, such as how to live their lives.

Codependents tend to give up and simply rely on the decisions of other people. They do not think about anything to avoid responsibility for their decisions. Oftentimes, their problem stems from childhood. Their parents may have indirectly or directly made them believe that they are not capable of making sound choices. They may have also been criticized by their decisions or made to think that they were stupid.

To overcome codependency, you have to have confidence in your mental ability. You can do this by treating your mind to some peace. You should learn how to stay calm and detach. Stop abusing your mind by constantly obsessing and worrying. Feed your mind with good information and healthy thoughts.

Day 17: Set Goals for Yourself

Codependents tend to lose themselves in their relationships. They treat their partner as a god or make them their world. This causes them to lose their own goals.

Healthy people set goals for themselves because they know that achieving something gives them a sense of fulfillment. They create their own happiness by pursuing their passions and accomplishing things.

Codependents, on the other hand, only aim to please their partners. They spend all their time and energy trying to do things for their partners because these people are the source of their happiness.

So, in order for you to overcome your codependency, you have to recover yourself. You have to set your own goals and do things that make you happy. Remember that you should do these things because you actually enjoy them and not because you want to impress your partner.

Do whatever you can, one day at a time. Set goals on a regular basis and check off the goals that you have completed. Think of your life before you met your partner. What were your dreams and ambitions back then? Start to live your life for you and not for your partner.

Day 18: Communicate Effectively

Codependents are incapable of proper communication. They often use words that please, manipulate, or control other people. When they communicate, their usual motives are to alleviate or cover up guilt. Their words reek of ulterior motives, repressed thoughts and feelings, shame, and low self-worth.

Codependents laugh when they want to cry. They claim to be fine when they are not. They allow themselves to be buried and bullied. They may even react inappropriately, as well as compensate, rationalize, and justify. They are not assertive. They threaten and badger, and then back down. They lie and become hostile. They apologize profusely and give hints to what they want.

Codependents are not direct. They do not say what they mean and do not mean what they say. They may not do this on purpose. It is simply the way they have learned how to communicate. They may have been raised to think that directly stating what they want is inappropriate or that saying 'no' is wrong.

If you want to improve your condition and no longer be a codependent, you should learn how to communicate properly. You should learn how to say 'no' when necessary. Recognize that your thoughts and feelings are valid and that you should not beat yourself up for having them. When you talk to other people, be straightforward. Do not beat around the bush and get upset when they do not get your hints.

Day 19: Complete a 12-Step Program

12-step programs, such as Alcoholics Anonymous, Narcotics Anonymous, and Overeaters Anonymous, operate on the same principles and rules. The members should admit that they have a problem and that their lives have become unmanageable due to their condition.

They should believe that there is a higher power that can help them restore their sanity. They should make decisions that can improve themselves and that they are prepared to eliminate the behaviors that cause them harm. They should also make amends to those they have hurt or negatively affected, as well as continue to take personal inventories. Furthermore, they should improve their consciousness and have a spiritual awakening.

12-step programs are not just self-help groups. They also teach people how to be happier, more successful, and more peaceful. They also promote healing. Joining a 12-step program allows you to meet people who are undergoing the same issues. They may not have the same exact problem as yours, but their situation can help you understand yours better. Being with these people can help you discuss your thoughts, feelings, and problems so that you can overcome your codependency.

Day 20: Stop the Drama

Some people get too engrossed in drama that the absence of it makes them uncomfortable. When things are going smoothly and perfectly, they start to create turmoil. Most codependents act this way because they are addicted to drama. They turn every little incident into a crisis.

According to Toby Rice Drews, author of Getting Them Sober, Volume II, codependents experience "excited misery" as a result of living with long term turmoil, misery, and crises. These people have become used to involving emotions with crises and problems that they tend to stay involved with issues that are not their concern. They may even create problems just to gain stimulation for themselves.

Codependents are comfortable in crisis. They feel void and empty when there is no drama. This behavior often causes them to end up with worse and bigger problems. So, if you want to overcome your codependency, you should aim to be drama-free. You have to understand that you do not have to create problems or be involved in the problems of others just to feel satisfied. If you want to fulfill your cravings for drama, you can get a job that excites you.

Did you enjoy this book so far?

Let me stop you for a moment. As a former codependent self-publisher, I have burning desire to give help and support to others who suffer from these issues alone, without guidance.

My goal and mission is to serve and inspire others to have more fulfilled, deeper and happier life.

I'd like to ask you to visit the Amazon Store and leave a honest review. It'd help my work and get this book to more who need it and I'd greatly appreciate it. Thank you!

Visit
www.amazon.com/dp/B077DXPXG1/
to leave a review on Amazon.

Day 21: Manage Expectations

Some people have a hard time dealing and managing expectations. This is especially true for codependents. Healthy people are able to let go and move on quickly when their expectations are not met.

Codependents, on the other hand, become upset and depressed. They also diminish their self-esteem. They tend to force their expectations on their partners. They try to control the outcomes of events. The more they try to be in control, the more often they fail. The more often they fail, the lower their self-worth gets. The lower their self-worth gets, the more they beat themselves up.

To overcome your codependency, you have to learn how to manage your expectations properly. Identify and examine them carefully. Discuss them with your partner to find out if you are both on the same page. If your expectations are not realistic or if your partner has different expectations, you can consider modifying them. However, make sure that you actually agree with the terms. Do not agree on anything just to please your partner.

Moreover, you should learn to let go of the outcome. Life is unpredictable. No matter what you do or how hard you prepare, you still cannot predict the future. So, you should stop getting anxious and learn to live in the present.

Day 22: Let Go of Your Fear for Intimacy

People need love. Codependents, however, often do not understand the true meaning of love. Some of them have a fear for intimacy. They feel that it is safer for them to stay alone or be in a relationship where they are not emotionally involved.

If you want to improve your life, you should be willing to take the risks that come with loving and being loved. Do not allow yourself to be trapped in a relationship that does not work just because you are afraid of the consequences of leaving. Let go of your fear to get close to people.

Day 23: Become Financially Responsible

A lot of codependents are financially dependent. At times, both partners agree to this setup. For example, the husband works to earn money for the family while the wife stays at home to take care of the children. There are also times when this kind of setup is not agreed upon.

Some codependents feel victimized and believe that they cannot take care of themselves financially. In the past, they may have been financially responsible. However, their current situation may have affected them and caused them to believe that they are no longer capable of being on their own.

You can overcome your codependency by becoming financially responsible. You can start working and earn your own money. When you experience financial freedom, you can achieve a sense of fulfillment. Then again, you should also learn that it is not healthy to be financially responsible for other people who do not take care of their own selves.

Day 24: Learn How to Forgive

Alcoholism and other compulsive disorders distort and twist good things, including forgiveness. Codependents are often bitter about their situation. They feel the need to take care of others but they also feel resentful when their good deeds are not acknowledged or returned.

You can overcome your codependency by learning how to forgive. You should forgive yourself so that you will no longer beat yourself up and feel not good enough. Likewise, you should forgive other people so that you can stop resenting them and no longer feeling hurt when they do not do what you expect them to do.

Day 25: Aim to Have Fun

Codependency and fun usually do not go together. Codependents find it hard to have fun because they are focused on hating themselves. They do not enjoy life because all they think about is their problems.

So, in order for you to get better, you should let go of the negative thoughts. Take a deep breath, relax, and think of the good things you have. Practice gratitude and be thankful for the blessings that you have in life. You may not always get what you want, but you still get positive outcomes.

Learn to enjoy yourself. Allow yourself to have fun once in a while. While it is true that your problems cannot magically go away, you can reduce your stress levels and clear your mind when you relax. This can help you come up with better decisions that can help solve your dilemmas.

Day 26: Set Boundaries

Codependents often experience issues with boundaries. In fact, most of them do not have boundaries. They do not know how far they should go. They do not know when they should stop being tolerant.

As a codependent, you have to know that compulsive disorders do not care about limits. They push boundaries and boldly step on them. So, in order for your condition and life to get better, you have to set boundaries for yourself and your relationship.

You should set a limit to what you should do and what you allow others to do for you. For example, you should no longer allow people to verbally or physically abuse you, lie to you, or use your money for addiction.

When you set your boundaries, make sure that you follow through. Stay firm. Say what you mean and mean what you say.

Day 27: Take Physical Care

It is common for codependents to neglect their grooming and health. Because they are so focused on taking care of others and giving them what they want, they forget to take care of their own needs.

Hence, you should start taking care of you. Do not think that you do not deserve to be cared for. If you are not feeling good, you should see a doctor. Take hot baths and pamper yourself.

Exercise and maintain a healthy diet. Get a haircut and wear clean clothes. Do not sacrifice your own health just to be there for others. You are important. You deserve to be cared for. Take care of your body.

Day 28: Get Professional Help If Necessary

You need to go to a professional if you are feeling depressed and contemplating suicide. You should also seek help from a professional if you want to stage an intervention for your alcoholic or drug addicted partner.

Likewise, you should get professional help if you suffered sexual or physical abuse or when you sexually or physically abuse your partner. You should also get professional help when you are no longer able to solve problems on your own or when you find yourself becoming addicted to alcohol or drugs.

Day 29: Learn About Strokes

No, this does not refer to the heart condition. Strokes is actually a term used in Transactional Analysis. It is about striving for healthy relationships. A healthy relationship involves giving and taking, respect, and other good qualities.

You are in a healthy relationship when you feel good and you find yourself achieving personal growth. As a codependent, you may not be familiar with healthy relationships. Thus, you have to learn more about them.

Do your research and seek counseling. Read books and articles written by experts. Once you learn about the elements of a healthy relationship, it would be easier for you to differentiate good and bad relationships. This would enable you to avoid suffering and becoming a codependent again in the future.

Day 30: Learn to Love and Live Again

Finally, you should learn to love and live again. Remember that there is always hope. You are not in a dead-end situation. You can get out of the unhealthy relationship you are in. You can seek help.

Codependents tend to believe that nobody will ever love them. They also feel the need to stay with their partners because they want to prove their love. However, if you want to overcome your codependency, you have to be strong and take the necessary actions. You need to stop the toxic cycle that you have.

You need to find and maintain a healthy balance in the different aspects of your life. You need to balance your physical and emotional needs. Recognize the fact that you are loveable and that you should not settle for less than what you know you deserve just because you are afraid of being on your own.

Conclusion

Now is the time to take action. If you did nothing more than just reading through this book, there is very little you can profit from the time you spent with it. In order to have a positive change in your life and relationships you must break your existing beliefs and habits and must get on a positive cycle. This. Is. Work.

I ask you to take seriously the ideas of this book, because if you don't, the codependency will chase you through your entire life. I recommend you to keep this book as a reference, a good compass on your journey. Also, you will need to have more in-depth understanding, self awareness and support.

Keep up the work!

I want to thank you for downloading my book, **The 30-Day Break Free Guide**! If you enjoyed it, then could you please take a minute and post an honest review about it on Amazon? I'd really appreciate it, as it will help me get my book out there to more people!

Visit the product page to leave a review on Amazon.com!

https://www.amazon.com/dp/B077DXPXG1/

Thank you and best wishes!

43781586R00035

Made in the USA
Lexington, KY
02 July 2019